A PEARL IN MY OYSTER

A Family's Journey through Addiction

C.B. Ennis

Copyright © 2023 C.B. Ennis
All rights reserved
First Edition

NEWMAN SPRINGS PUBLISHING
320 Broad Street
Red Bank, NJ 07701

First originally published by Newman Springs Publishing 2023

ISBN 978-1-68498-925-6 (Paperback)
ISBN 978-1-68498-926-3 (Digital)

Printed in the United States of America

I dedicate this book to my mother Catherine Greene Brannon. The poem she wrote is the inspiration for the title. She was a daughter, sister, wife, mother, grandmother and great grandmother. But above all, she was a Christian. She talked the talk and walked the narrow path.

My mother was a prayer warrior, and she believed in having faith in all situations no matter how dire or extreme. She was an encouragement to all and always practiced listening and loving in the flesh not from a distance. She instilled in me confidence and strength living in a fallen world. She loved people of all kinds with her whole heart.

Her very personal story is told in a chapter of this book. It was one of the hardest chapters to write. My hope is her love for writing and her love for God will shine through the pages of this book. I just wish she could be here to witness this in person.

Casey's grandmother was the pivotal person who ultimately caused change in his life for the better. She was the driving force that kept him alive during the dark days of addiction. I owe her so much, and my hope is her life will not be forgotten but glorified through this book until I see her in Heaven one day.

Acknowledgments

This book is a combined effort of so many people who sacrificed their time and resources to help me make this dream come true. Jesus Christ whispered in my ear many years ago to write this book, but the hectic day-to-day of a full-time job, raising kids, and many other endless responsibilities made it seem like a distant dream.

When I made the decision to retire from teaching in January of 2020, I knew that I had to take this God-ordained assignment seriously. I announced my intentions to my family at Christmas of 2019. Their initial response was disbelief. I asked for a laptop for Christmas, and I got that gift from my family. I am so grateful for their continued support and encouragement through this process.

To my husband Steve, I want to thank you for your patience and understanding of my struggles with technology at times. You made sacrifices so that my passion for this book became a reality. I appreciate the countless hours you have spent helping me navigate the many paths of technology, how to save and store files, and how to change the interface so my editor could edit the pages successfully.

To my son and the topic of this book, I am grateful for your willingness to share your story with the public so that others can find hope through addiction. I am so very proud of the man you are becoming and cannot wait to see what God has planned for the future.

To my daughter Kelsey, I hope that you will find healing and forgiveness through these pages. I appreciate the chapter you shared from the perspective of a little sister, and I pray the healing process will continue for you throughout the future. It is my hope that, in time, you and Casey will find a common ground and be able to have a relationship one day.

I am so grateful for my editor and mentor Susan Smith. As an amateur writer with no experience, she has been extremely helpful and supportive throughout the process of writing the book. Susan is an English professor at the Southern Baptist Seminary. She even made an effort to meet me in person to share breakfast and talk about the book. It was an honor and privilege to work with her so closely. She sacrificed her time and efforts to help me navigate this unknown territory.

I would also like to acknowledge my neighbors and friends Rodger and Janet Sauls. They wrote and had their first book published: *Just Trust Me, Love God*. Sharing their book with me and talking through the process led me to examine the possibility of following in their footsteps and with Jesus guiding my words and steps to obedience, I too could write a book. Their encouragement and guidance along the way has given me the resolve to stay the course and to ask questions if in doubt. It was such a relief to know Rodger and Janet were available at any time along this journey. They mentored me and reminded me of the importance of this book and the hope it could bring to others.

Last but not least, I would like to thank Janie Cassady, my publication coordinator, and the editing team for your patience and commitment with an inexperienced writer and for allowing our story to be told.

Introduction

The title of this book is *A Pearl in my Oyster: A Family's Journey through Addiction*. It comes from a poem my mother wrote to her grandson Casey. This book is dedicated to her in her honor. She enjoyed writing and expressed her love, joy, and disappointments throughout her life through her poetry. Little did she know, how real her precious words on paper would become a predictor of our son's future. The oyster is a mollusk that is a bottom feeder. It sucks up all the debris from the ocean floor taking it back into the shell. Approximately, one out of ten thousand oysters will have the rare opportunity to encounter a small grain of sand that can make a home between the opening of the shell and the mantle inside. Over a long period of time, even decades, an occasional pearl will be naturally created inside the hard shell. It is a very rare event, but it can happen. The pearl is a treasure inside a harsh and dirty environment.

The pearl represents the beautiful transformation that occurs over time as God works in and through the life of an addict in a supernatural way. Those who are strong enough to endure the years of torture and darkness and fight the good fight have the rare opportunity of encountering such a beautiful and rare treasure. Unfortunately, this event is so rare that there are very few that do survive to tell their stories. They are left with broken pieces and families that have to accept the reality of never seeing their loved ones again. It is a grim reality that many will face in our communities. Addiction does not discriminate. Any socioeconomic group can and will encounter this *monster*. The evil *monster* will come to steal, kill, and destroy life. The war is real, but our message is the battle can be won!

I decided to write this book because, years ago, as I struggled with living in the midst of addiction, Jesus spoke to me in the darkness and said, "Tell your story." So on that very day, I decided to put every word, feeling, heartache, and emotion on paper. As the months of suffering turned into years, the voice got stronger and more persistent: "Write your story!" I had accumulated ten journals that I put my blood, sweat, and tears into. I never questioned my God and the assignment he had for me. I was just obedient. I thought of my mother's favorite verse from **John 15:5: "I am the vine you are the branches, abide in me and bear much fruit."**

During the dark days of addiction, I summoned all the prayer warriors I could find. The more I wrote, the more empowered I felt. I no longer suffer in silence. I began to put on the armor of God and fight back with everything I had. I recall the scripture from **Ephesians 6:11. It says, "Put on the full armor of God so that you will be able to stand firm against the schemes of the devil."** I had an up close and personal encounter one day as I looked my son in the eyes; I saw evilness that shook me to my core. In that moment, with stern resolve and conviction, I said in an uncontrollable rage, "I will *not* sell your soul to the devil!" From that day forward, I was determined that God would be by my side as we battled this *monster* together and not allow my one and only son to be destroyed by addiction. After all, he is a child of God; he was created in his image. His life was worth saving. God had plans for him to prosper, and I would do everything in my power to make sure that happened. I held on to this scripture during the uncertain days: **Jeremiah 29:11, "For I know the plans I have for you, declares the Lord, plans to prosper you and not harm you, plans to give you a hope and a future."** This journey that we were about to embark on opened my eyes to the power of scripture and prayer through difficult times.

No one has to suffer in silence and be ashamed to talk about their feelings, emotions, and struggles. This book is a testament that anyone can survive addiction when and if Jesus is leading the way and there are tough love principles in place. But as I learned the hard way, the battle can only be won when the family sets necessary boundaries and does not enable the addict to continue feeding the *monster* with comforts, money, and resources. I truly believe that our family did not go through this experience for nothing. I believe that God knew from the beginning that this situation would lead to something bigger than me. A family must stand firm in unity and agree to fight together. Consistency is the key to winning the battle. The life lessons we have endured have not been in vain if just one family member of the addict will read this book and share and give hope where there seems to be no hope in sight.

That voice of my Master says with a strong conviction, "*Write your book* to give hope to the hopeless."

My Casey Boy

You are the pearl in my oyster, sir
Glistening like the new dewdrop on a cat's fur
The stare of those beautiful blue eyes compels
The relentless pearl as it cast a spell
Then quickly like the rising sun
You smile with dancing eyes of fun
You're growing faster than any weed
Cause you're my pearl in my oyster feed
Pearls capture attention wherever they go
Just like Casey—how we love you so
You're practicing that swing to the left, you know
Be it after a bull or roping a cow so low
You're still the pearl in the oyster, Casey Boy
As you glow and gleam far prettier than any toy
I know you cannot stay so innocent and pure
Unless you reach for God's hand, not worldly lure
Somehow, I just know deep inside my heart
With godly guidance of your parents, you'll not depart
The pearl in my oyster you will always be
God sent us an angel named Casey, you see

Your loving and doting grandmother,

Catherine G. Brannon
12-12-93

In the Beginning

The title of this book is very unusual and different, I admit, but the meaning behind it is anything but. *A Pearl in My Oyster* is based on a grandmother's love of writing poetry and sharing it with others. Once upon a time, the doting grandmother of Casey Ennis created a poem: "My Casey Boy." The title of the poem was originated from her own perceptions and observations as she welcomed Casey into the world on a moonlit night on July 3, 1993. That night, I was in the hospital room with much anticipation of the arrival of my firstborn child. With my husband, Steve, me, and the soon-to-be grandmothers of this precious first born, I eagerly prepared to give birth to my son. Every bit of the labor process went as planned.

This precious baby was born healthy. He was a beautiful baby with blonde hair and big blue eyes. He weighed eight pounds and four ounces, was healthy as a horse, and had no medical problems. I was so thankful to give birth to such a beautiful and healthy baby boy, and we named him Casey Doyle Ennis. Casey, after the famous baseball's Hall of Fame player that struck out time and time again but never gave up! With bases loaded, Casey Stengel hit a home run that no one expected, and he became the hero of the game. My husband Steve dreamed of the day his son would play baseball and love the game as much as he did as a child! Steve had so many hopes and dreams for his firstborn son, and he anxiously waited for the day he would put his first bat in his hand.

His childhood was relatively typical. At his health checkup appointments, Casey was always off the charts for height and weight, and the pediatricians warned me he would be very tall one day. At times, throughout his childhood, I noticed he was very curious and stubborn about having his way. Like most mothers, I thought this was pretty typical. Casey was an adorable child with a delightful personality. Early on, it was clear he was very smart and inquisitive. He took risks sometimes that kept me on guard and constantly keeping him close by my side. Casey seemed to cross boundaries, not to be defiant and dangerous but more out of curiosity and exploring his world around him.

When Casey was a baby, and just beginning to roll and show signs of wanting to move I lovingly placed in the center of our king-sized bed and to my surprise, he would roll over enough times to get to the side of the bed in seconds. I would gasp as he reached the edge. I never let him hit the floor, but he came pretty close at times. I found out pretty quickly this boy wanted to move and needs supervision at all times. The bouncy chair and swing that attached to the doorway would soon become his best friends. He would bounce for hours and swing through the air like he was flying. Casey seemed to be the happiest when he was not confined to a space but had mobility at all times to give him the freedom to be a lively, energic little boy. He met all of the milestones as an average baby would, so we felt confident he would be healthy and strong. He had chunky little legs that carried him wherever his heart desired and learned pretty quickly just how far he could go without getting hurt.

He listened to corrections from his parents and would react accordingly, but once in a while, he would get this look in his eye that said, "I want to test the limits," and most of the time, the result was not good, and the end result was correction or punishment.

Casey was not much of a sleeper at night. He would wake up several times to be fed or held and rocked back to sleep. He would almost always drift off just for a few seconds, and as I walked over to place him in the crib, the movement would wake him up. I can recall many nights crawling on my hands and knees out of the nursery only to be startled by a cry that could be heard all over the neighborhood. Casey would stand up holding the sides of the crib crying real tears in the middle of the night. The exhaustion was paralyzing, and only new parents can understand the level of exhaustion we experienced.

The only time Casey would rest is in the car as we shuttled from place to place. Unfortunately, I could not be in the car on autopilot and take a nap with him. Nap time was a challenge, among other things, as we embarked on the journey of parenthood.

One of those days stands out in my mind vividly. The events of that day were horrific and stressful. On this particular day, Casey was in the second grade, and there was a reading contest taking place at his elementary school. So he wanted every ribbon he earned for reading books pinned neatly on the front side of his T-shirt.

There was a special assembly in the auditorium to announce the winners for the most books read for each grade level. Casey was very competitive and confident he would surely win. As the classes lined up to go into the assembly, there was an unexpected turn of events, and it was suddenly canceled. Well, that did not set well with Casey, so out of anger and frustration, he took one of the ribbons off, walked over to the wall socket in the hallway, and proceeded to put the safety pin in the electrical socket. Unfortunately, he picked the active socket and proceeded to light up as sparks traveled through his fingertips up his arm.

The teacher and support staff quickly got the other students to safety while Casey was whisked off to the office. The entire school was on lockdown. The firetrucks and emergency medical team came out to investigate. As a mother, I was horrified to receive that call. The call was from the school secretary, and she announced that there had been an emergency, and we needed to come immediately to the school. At the time, I was working as a teacher in North Raleigh, and it was not easy to navigate through the traffic. I prayed to God that my little son was alive.

When I arrived, about the same time as Steve, we both held on tight to each other hand in hand. As we entered the building with the fire department blocking the sidewalk and standing by, I felt so many different emotions at one time. As we rushed to the front office, we were met with the principal who looked like she was in shock and had seen a ghost! She very calmly described the events that led up to an electrocution! I remember being in shock and could not wrap my brain around why Casey would do such a thing!

The principal took us to where Casey was hovering over a sink throwing up. The tips of his fingers were charred black like a piece of hot coal smoldering on a grill with smoke lingering; Casey was in pain, and he was very upset. He stated through his heavy breathing and panting that he was upset about the reading challenge assembly being canceled, and he acted on impulse. I felt like this was not real, and I did not know whether to hug him or scream out loud! I was relieved that he was alive after being electrocuted. This little boy in the second grade had acted impulsively, and out of disappointment and anger, he thought it was a good idea to put a safety pin in an electrical socket and shut down an entire school?

As a lesson learned in the hardest way possible, the principal suggested that because of his age, she did not feel that suspension from school was a reasonable punishment; therefore, she wanted to take a different approach. She wanted Casey to speak to his fellow students about his mistake and what he learned from the experience. So Casey, being branded physically and mentally, had to face his teachers and peers as he suffered the embarrassment of explaining why he caused the entire school to be shut down that very fine day. That was sufficient punishment for a little boy in the second grade. In hindsight, this was a big red flag that we needed to pay attention to as our son continued through his early years.

The rest of his elementary experience was pretty typical. After second grade, his teacher raised a flag of concern regarding Casey's reading ability. She said he was slightly delayed and needed some extra work over the summer. That year, I took on a new teaching assignment in North Raleigh and decided it would be best to transfer both Casey and Kelsey, our daughter, with me to a new school for a fresh start.

That summer, I spent many hours working with Casey on comprehension skills because, as a certified teacher, I knew the importance of these critical reading skills. If he was delayed in this area, we needed to work hard and get his reading level up to grade level before transferring schools. A part of me wondered, *did the impact of electrocution affect his brain in some way?* At a very early age, I read to both of my children, and we enjoyed many nights of reading bedtime stories. That love for reading was instilled in both of my children before they entered school.

I had Casey tested in the area of reading to make sure he was on grade level as he entered the third grade in a new school with new peers. The tests showed that the hard work in the summer prior to his third-grade year was successful. Not only was Casey reading and comprehending on grade level but also his comprehension skills were above the average mean. This put my mind at ease, and the rest of his elementary years in a school environment seemed to come and go with no other earth-shattering events.

As the middle school year approached, I started to notice that Casey associated himself with older peers. As the doctor warned, Casey would be that kid that would be very tall and big, just like his dad. He went through an awkward time in which he gained weight and seemed to explode in height. This is when I started to notice a definite change in his personality and independence. He became more defiant and rebellious at times. He was the tween that all of the girls liked because he had a charming, friendly personality.

As Casey neared high school, he often associated with others who were several years older than him. It was during this awkward time in his development that he started to be dishonest. I noticed he was lying about where he would go and what he was doing. He became a bit rebellious at times; he rebelled against most anything and everything. Desperately trying to find his own identity, mom and dad were no longer the most important influences in his life. He looked to his social circle of friends for advice in life circumstances. This was a trying time for our family. He started to test the boundaries and even take unnecessary risks along the way. His relationship with his parents and little sister had changed in a negative way. Casey was cruel to his little sister; it broke my heart to see how he treated her. She wanted so badly to be protected and loved by her big brother, but Casey was self-centered and had no time for her. She was too young to understand the separation that was happening without any explanation.

On one particular day, we were scheduled for a family photo session, and Casey had not had his hair cut in a very long time. He refused to do it for the photo and turned it into a power struggle that caused us a great deal of stress. Finally, he said his grandmother could trim his hair, but only her, and then he would agree to go and smile like a good child for the camera. He lived up to his side of the bargain, but his smile was not genuine, and he was not very cooperative throughout the process. From that day forward, there were red flags that these tween years would be both turbulent and difficult to navigate as parents.

I read every book I could find and talked to professionals about strong-willed children and how to break them. We consulted the professionals in child psychiatry. It did not seem to matter. Casey always seemed to stay one step ahead of us, and he was very convincing and manipulative. It made parenting feel very uncertain and uncomfortable. We were definitely out of our league and over our heads as we desperately tried to navigate the arena of parenting. All of the professionals who would assess him would say, "Casey is dangerously smart for his age; he is very manipulative." "Casey is very curious and will test the limits and take risks." Boundaries did not work, and he was the captain of his own destiny. We had very little influence on Casey's decisions, behaviors, or actions. It was a very frustrating and dangerous place to be as parents. The questions that remained unanswered kept me up at night and caused me to have a lot of anxiety.

The sequence of events was just foreshadowing of the turbulent years that followed. None could prepare us for the road and battle ahead of us.

Freedom Comes at a Price

Casey attended both middle school and high school close to home in Johnston County as I took positions as a teacher in this county. I always believed that it was better to have both of my children close by where I could keep an eye on them and help them if needed. That decision would prove to be very challenging as Casey transitioned into high school in the local area. Casey was involved in social clubs and activities, and he was also on the school baseball team. His freshman and sophomore years were pretty typical. He did well in his classes, and his teachers and peers seem to like and respect him. He was even nominated for the homecoming court, and as his mother, I had the honor of being his escort on the homecoming court on the football field. It was a great honor to be nominated by his peers, and I was very proud of him. How could things go so wrong so quickly as he forged on as a junior in high school?

During the summer between his sophomore and junior year, it was clear he was growing up too quickly, and his desires for baseball, scouts, and other past times would be a thing of the past. As soon as he got his driver's license, he had plans to conquer the world. Finally, he had the freedom to come and go as he pleased without parents hovering over him. We made the biggest mistake of our lives by buying him a used red Chevrolet truck. Reluctantly, we gave him the keys and the freedom he desired. Casey was the master of convincing us of his intentions and actions. He convinced us he could be trusted when we had a good gut feeling he may not be trustworthy.

Buying a truck for Casey to drive proved to be a mistake that snowballed into a disaster. Even though we had him sign a contract with rules for operation including what the law would require and for our expectation of the truck's use, Casey did not take this seriously and clearly had his own agenda. In his mind, he was free as a bird, and he had no intentions of honoring a piece of paper with arbitrary rules. Within a few weeks, he had his first wreck, and he had repeatedly ignored warnings to stay within the law and our expectations. He should have lost his privileges. I felt so anxious and unprepared for how he tested and crossed every boundary we put in front of him to keep him safe and out of trouble.

We educated Casey with the process of making a vehicle purchase. We used some cash and borrowed money from our bank with him present for this process. After the purchase was completed, Steve rode with Casey driving back to Garner. They stopped into our local car insurance office to share the purchase information with them. Our insurance rep spoke with Casey about driving at sixteen and safety and procedures of the road. Steve and I stood in solidarity! We were determined that there would be consequences and accountability that went along with the freedom of driving. I wondered why he would not follow our rules. I wondered why he could not be like other teens who didn't push their parents' parameters.

As I pondered these questions and observed Casey's behavior, it was crystal clear that something was going on with him. There was an underlying difference. It became very difficult to motivate him to rise and shine for school. He often missed school because of a sudden illness. He skipped classes and hung out with the wrong group of teens that had no goals or ambition. He began to associate with people who were known for using and selling drugs. I tried to get him to talk to me, but he refused. He kept silent and blamed us for being overprotective and trying to interfere with his social life. This time was both frustrating and embarrassing. The result of this is that I could not separate my personal life from my professional life as a teacher because they were intertwined in a way that caused me great anxiety and frustration. I can remember chasing him down the school hallways as Casey tried to skip school. I felt powerless to stop his reckless behavior! I spoke to his counselor and spent many days sitting in his office to dissect my own feelings of hopelessness and being on the edge of a breakdown. I was bound and determined to get Casey through high school with a diploma if it killed both of us. I often had thoughts of being fired because I had spent too much time and energy trying to keep Casey inside the school building. I had a very difficult time focusing on my own teaching responsibilities.

On April 15, 2010, my daughter's birthday, Casey drove to school and parked in the junior's parking lot. He went in to the student services office and announced he was late and needed a note to enter his first block class. The receptionist smelled marijuana and noticed his behavior seemed erratic and unusual. Within a few minutes after I entered the school building, I was called to the main office. There sitting in her office was Casey. It was early morning around 7:00 a.m. I thought, *Why in the world is Casey in trouble at this hour of the morning?* The assistant principal said that Casey came to school under the influence of a controlled substance, and he would need to search Casey's vehicle. I was shocked and in disbelief!

The school resource officer, assistant principal, and others proceeded to walk out to his truck in the parking lot. We discovered Casey was under the influence and had been careless enough to leave marijuana and drug paraphernalia in his vehicle. My worst fears came true. My son, Casey Ennis, would soon be arrested and taken to jail for possession of a controlled substance on school campus. The school resource officer was empathetic enough to avoid more embarrassment by engaging the handcuffs outside in the parking lot. That day, Casey was fingerprinted and labeled a criminal. He was taken to the Johnston County Jail as a minor offender.

I waged war within myself as I pondered over whether to let him stay in jail or bail him out. Because it was his sister's birthday, and we did not want to break this bad news on her special day, Steve and I agreed we would bail him out and try to put it behind us for the sake of his sister. Casey was relieved but not remorseful. The joy of his sister's birthday was spoiled because we had to bail him out of jail. At this time, she was in eighth grade at the middle school and lived under his name and influence as his little sister. She was humiliated and embarrassed in the worst possible way. That day is one we will never forget.

This single incident was only the beginning of his encounter with the legal system. It was clear that Casey was heading down the wrong path and had to be stopped. At his own persuasion, he suggested to us that he apply for a job at a local fast-food restaurant nearest the school. We thought this would be a diversion from the dangerous path he was on and give him a sense of responsibility. It seemed like a rational response to a hopeless situation. What we know now, as we look back, is that Casey gradually became a master of manipulation and told us exactly what we wanted to hear to continue to live this way without punishment and disruption of his disastrous lifestyle.

Like many other teenagers, he often worked after school and on weekends, and from what he shared with us, he seemed to be doing well at his new job. We sacrificed changes in our work schedules and routines; we even sacrificed our much-needed sleep. During this time, Casey lied and schemed to continue to use and acquire drugs at work. To my knowledge this is where Casey was introduced to cocaine and very quickly became addicted to this drug. We were quickly able to determine this based on his unusual behaviors. He began having issues sleeping and would often stay awake for days at a time. He wasn't interested in eating and his behavior was erratic. This took a toll on his physical and mental health. His once-healthy body dwindled down to bones. As he craved the drug more and more, his paycheck began to diminish. Casey was hooked on cocaine. We were appalled to learn that his manager was the one who introduced him to the drug and the one supplying him. They would often use together while working the night shift. How could this happen? He had lied and made us believe he was working hard as an employee of the well-known fast-food chain.

As a mother, I was outraged by this injustice perpetrated and carried out by the assistant manager, an adult in a role as a supervisor. After the facts came to light, I confronted the manager in person. Casey and the assistant manager were fired immediately, and the authorities were called. How could a person in a position of authority consciously justify getting a naive young kid addicted to cocaine?

The moment of truth had arrived and Casey had to face the monster and tell us the truth. His grades suffered and his behaviors were erratic and unpredictable. Steve and I had to find a place where he could be assessed and evaluated for substance abuse. This demon, called addiction, had wreaked havoc on our lives, and we were desperate for help.

I vividly remember one night that we were called to rescue Casey from his bad choices. As we were riding down the road in the car with a *monster* in the back, yelling and being irrational, a defining moment occurred where I had enough! I declared to Steve, "If you take him back to our home, I will leave because I cannot take it anymore!" That was a breaking point for me! Steve looked at me with all seriousness and said, "Okay, but where will we take him for the night?" We decided together at that moment that we had to be unified to fight this *monster* called addiction. We drove to a hospital that treats Psychiatric disorders and addictions. The ride there was torture. Casey went crazy and tried to jump out of a moving car. When we arrived, it was a fight to get him out of the car. We fought with him, and in that fight, Casey tore the car door panel off and broke Steve's glasses as he fought for his freedom. We had to go inside and ask the staff to take him anyway they could. The staff came out with Tasers and shocked him with a force that knocked him to the ground.

Once admitted, he underwent psychiatric evaluations, among many others, to determine the best treatment options. He was stripped of everything and placed in isolation. The evaluations were conducted over days and were deemed to be conclusive. Casey was diagnosed with cyclothymic disorder, oppositional defiant disorder, and polysubstance abuse. What in the world does all of that mean in layman's terms? Basically, Casey has a mild form of bipolar that, by definition, is "highs and lows" in mood that are milder than bipolar. He can function in society most of the time. The oppositional defiant disorder is the ability to manipulate and deceive others, and this explained why when things did not go his way, he would act out in anger and frustration. His cognitive abilities were assessed and found to be normal and rational when substances were not involved.

Suggested interventions included inpatient long-term care for substance abuse and medication for the cyclothymic disorder. Wow! That sounded reasonable, and we had no alternative but to trust the professionals.

A plan was made, and Casey had a diagnosis and treatment. For the first time in a long time, I could breathe. I was relieved that we were finally on the right track. At the very least, we had some sort of answers and a path to follow toward sobriety! When we entered this secure facility for the first time, it felt cold and dark. Bars were on the windows and some patients were restrained. Due to his age and being a minor there were very few options available to us. Inpatient facilities that treat addiction were very challenging to find in our state and so we had to look at other options. Casey walked in with no socks or shoes. We were told that they did not want to give him anywhere to stash drugs or weapons. I was a little uncomfortable, and Steve and Kelsey felt the same. We met with the professionals in a secure room where we decided that Casey needed to go from there to a facility in Tennessee. We had a plan and needed to make it happen soon. There was urgency to this matter! The staff agreed.

How did we come up with the idea to send Casey to New Life Lodge, a facility in the remote mountains of Tennessee? Soon after that time Casey spent at the facility, Steve and I began to seek inpatient facilities for Casey to take him out of Johnston County and the life he was determined to destroy. We spent day and night doing research and talking on the phone. We located a place in the mountains of Tennessee. It is a very remote area with intense counseling and group therapy centered around addiction.

Off we went to this remote location that took all day to travel in hopes to help Casey regain his life. It was a long ride, but it was needed. We rode with hope and anticipation for Casey to have a changed life—the "new life" the title of the lodge suggested.

During this thirty-day inpatient care for Casey's addiction, Steve and I attended counseling too as we knew we needed to deal with our own feelings and the impact this awful disease had on us as individuals and a couple. The counseling was helpful, and I felt a sense of relief because for at least thirty days, I could at least breathe and find some sense of peace. I researched any and all resources to try to make sense of this unexpected turn of events that we were not prepared for nor had a clue how to cope. To my surprise, there were very few books written about addiction or materials. There were no autobiographies. I wondered why and began to pray a lot. In my quiet time and calm hours my mind was always focused on what I could do to stop this vicious cycle. Surely, I could find answers to this dilemma. Didn't I have control over this disease? In the darkest of times, I spent many sleepless nights praying and weeping. One night, I heard a small voice that said, "*Write your story.*" At that time, I did not have the motivation or energy to do this. However, I began to keep journals where my pain and agony was poured out on paper. Every event, along with every heartache, was journaled. The voice was indeed the voice of my Heavenly Father and Savior.

The weeks that Casey spent at an inpatient facility was a time for me to write, pray, and try to make sense of this unwelcome *monster* that had turned our lives upside down and inside out. We were invited to come for a parent weekend at the facility, and of course, we made sacrifices to be there to see our son and learn more about addiction. This is a family disease, and we were all negatively impacted, so we talked to Kelsey, and she agreed to come as well.

I learned a lot and had hope for the first time that maybe this experience would be the defining moment in time that would change Casey's path. His counselors spoke highly of Casey and said he has benefited from being there. He was even able to finish his high school classes to receive credit for his junior year. He was released to us with a continuing plan of outpatient treatment at home. This sounded reasonable, and Casey agreed.

Unfortunately, it was not long before we were once again manipulated and lied to as the pattern of addictive behavior continued shortly after being released from that New Life Lodge. Casey lied to the counselors and played their game to be released. Casey was a master at manipulation and deception, and he was smart enough to do just enough to win their approval and outsmart the professionals. This was beyond frustrating on so many levels, and we walked many steps back to square 1 with no answers. Casey wore us out physically and mentally, and he slowly, but surely, stole from us.

He continued to lie to us and made a mockery of our ability to parent him. In desperation, we kicked him out of our house and our lives. We simply had nothing left to give. No amount of unconditional love and courage could convince us to continue to live like prisoners in our own home. He moved in with a guy who made it easy for Casey to continue his lifestyle as a drug addict. Steve and I had feelings of hope when he was at the facility which soon turned in to feelings of hopelessness, desperation, and isolation. We barely had enough energy to keep our marriage intact or continue to work. My Heavenly Father had to carry me during this time because I was so depressed and felt absolutely drained and hopeless.

The poem "Footprints in the Sand" became my reality, and I prayed for God to carry me through this season. I was embarrassed to talk to others and stood in judgment from my own daughter and some friends. My daughter was forced to stay places other than her own home. My faith was almost nonexistent, and constant prayers for healing from addiction seemed to fall on deaf ears and unanswered. I only had a mustard seed of faith, and it was obvious. My physical and mental health was impacted, and at times, I just honestly did not want to live another day in the shadow of addiction. There was a war going on in my heart and head because as much as I hated to put him out of our home, I knew that the consequences of staying would be irreversible.

Casey was suspended part of his senior year and spent most of his senior year of high school at an alternative school. He took his remaining classes behind bars and supervised at all times during school hours at a place called South Campus. Steve and I had to adjust our schedules to get Casey to and from this facility. Casey was not allowed to set foot on the school campus and had to get special permission to present his senior project to a few counselors so he could earn his diploma. We pushed him to do this and were thankful they would allow this one opportunity.

Eventually, Casey was sent back to his high school for his senior year, and he continued to defy the rules. Subsequently, Casey had harsh words with the principal. This was the last straw, and the principal expelled him and refused to allow him to walk across the stage to receive his diploma. What a blow! That was one of my lowest points in this journey. I had to somehow accept the fact that my son would not walk across the stage with his peers to accept his diploma. I tried to fight it, but ultimately, I knew he had disrespected his school and his community and did not deserve this opportunity. It was a crushing blow to Steve and me. It was very hard to process as I experienced feelings of anger, resentment, and unrecognizable hurt—the kind of hurt that caused excruciating pain that would paralyze me. "Is this really what God wants for Casey's life?" I often asked myself. A sequence of events where this *monster* called addiction came to steal, kill, and destroy Casey's life? I could not accept that, and I cried out to God in desperation: "Lord, will you stop this destructive pattern of behavior? Can you hear my cries for help?"

For years, Casey lived with other friends. He was no longer welcome in our home as long as he continued to use drugs. Casey was never homeless because he had so many friends in low places, and people who would take him in temporarily. The professionals insisted that he figure out life on his own without any support from his family. We loved Casey from a distance but had to set boundaries so that he did not destroy us and suck us into his irrational world of addiction. The professionals would say, "You have to let Casey hit rock bottom." Casey had hit walls, was kicked out of school, was arrested, and was jailed. Where in the world was his bottom? What would it take to change this path? This path allowed the devil to be the captain of Casey's ship and guide his destiny.

It is hard to admit, but Steve and I wanted to have a relationship so badly with our son that we continued to allow addiction to creep into our lives and allow us to be sucked in and tortured time and time again. The worst days and darkest times occurred in his early twenties beginning in 2010. He met someone that was older, and they embarked on a new journey as the alcohol, marijuana, and cocaine were just not enough anymore. Casey and this individual got involved with one of the deadliest of *monsters*; this *monster* is called opioids.

The two got the drugs from a family member who was paralyzed and took the medicine for pain. It seemed harmless at first, but it was not harmless at all. This person gave the appearance of someone who genuinely cared about Casey and was going to be a true friend. All along, his objective was selfish and dangerous. He claimed he worked in the "bread business," and it was very profitable. I did not question it at first. The real truth was he was selling his disabled aunt's medication and profiting for himself.

Much later, my daughter said Casey was stashing the money in secret hiding places all over the house. Casey once again found himself addicted to the opioid *monster*. He was addicted and physically sick when he did not have them in his system. I recall days he would not eat because the drug suppressed his appetite so severely. On the rare occasion he did eat, it usually had a bad outcome. We witnessed Casey throwing up entire plates of food. He was literally a skeleton chasing the next high. Casey was scared to be without the drug because he would be so physically sick.

He spent the next few years estranged from us as his parents. He lived the life of a desperate addict looking for the next high. Occasionally, I called, and Casey would be happy to hear my voice. Casey says now that it was my prayers and encouragement that kept him alive during those dark times. My encouragement and calm voice gave him hope to live. I always had horrible visions of his death, and I had to fight those images to move toward the light. The light was dim, but it was still on, and as long as Casey had a mustard seed of faith and still breathing, I knew he had a chance. The devil wanted to steal, kill, and destroy all hope, and he wanted to destroy our relationship. I guess that is why we held on so tightly to Casey because we could not fathom the thought of burying our son.

Steve and I lived with the reality every day that our son might not live to see another day, and that *fear was paralyzing*! In the midst of this, Casey once again was forced to accept the fact that he needed intervention and treatment. On a spring afternoon, the same day we received a call that Kelsey was accepted to East Carolina University, another call was devastating. Casey was arrested for a felony of manufacturing and selling a controlled substance. The bad news rocked our world again, and we had to struggle to celebrate the good news of our daughter's college acceptance. Off to jail Casey went, but this time, we did not bail him out. He had to suffer the consequences of his own behavior. He was incarcerated again but this time with his partner in crime. Casey kept his sanity by talking to us by phone and seeing us during the limited hours of visitation privileges.

At this point of another arrest and imprisonment of my son, I experienced a unique irony. During this time of Casey's incarceration, I too was imprisoned. It was not a physical prison that I was in; it was a mental prison because I did not know what to do or which way to turn. I did not want to tell too many people, who could have prayed for and with me, because I was ashamed and knew my family would be judged. The only One I knew who had the answers was the only one I could really trust at that time.

Like the Apostle Paul, I knew what it was like to live "behind bars" (though my bars were not physical like Paul's imprisonment). Only Jesus could help. Just as the Apostle Paul wrote during his time in jail to the churches he helped to establish and cared very much for, I also wrote during my time in the mental jail because I continued to love and care very much for my son and the whole family. I only wanted what was best for them in the eyes of the Lord as Paul wanted the best for the churches he established and served. Though I did not always know how to express exactly how I was feeling, I wanted to chronicle the events because I had a hope—a hope that, one day, I could share my writing with someone…anyone…who may also be in "chains" and desire freedom as I did then, much like Paul's letters from jail are still read to give us encouragement in times of suffering.

Though I felt I was chained in an emotional prison of my own, I had to carry on during more difficult circumstances. Since Casey had been living with his girlfriend, we had the embarrassing task of going to her parents' home to get his personal belongings. Her father was very agitated and blamed Casey for the arrests. They made the decision to remove Casey from their home considering these circumstances.

The Battle

Casey's behaviors became increasingly erratic and dangerous. He would reach a boiling point very quickly, and there was no calming him down. I looked my son in the eyes and did not recognize the face staring back at me because of the *monster* he had become. When Casey lost himself, he would act out physically in fits of anger and frustration. He would engage in these scare tactics. The drugs would dictate his behavior. He could not be reasoned with nor did Casey have the ability to problem solve in normal situations. His erratic behavior became more often and more dangerous every time. We called the police at times and all they would say is, "I am sorry; we cannot do anything because he is a minor and under your guardianship." This confirmed that we were stuck with this unrecognizable *monster*, and there was absolutely nothing we could do to make things any better. It was like being trapped and imprisoned in our own home. There was no escape, exit door, or relief in sight.

After being released from jail he was ordered by the courts to go into an inpatient facility once again to detox and get clean from opioid addiction. He stayed at the Wilmington Treatment Center for less than thirty days and seemed to get the help and guidance he needed. The medical staff even recommended an injection that would curb his cravings for opiates. Many of his closest friends had lost their battle with addiction and died. Casey was one of the few who was left to fight this *monster*. Apparently, it continues to be an evil thing that has taken the lives of young people in our community. Every month there is a young person overdosing on lethal drugs. It was evil for my family, and it continues to be an evil force impacting our communities. I lived my life in a constant fear of losing my one and only son. Just like before, as long as he was removed from the toxic environment and within the confines of a treatment facility he was clean and back to his old self temporarily or so we thought.

Unfortunately though, the cravings continued after Casey left the treatment center, and the cravings were too strong to ignore. We took Casey back to the facility where he would get the injection to curb his opiod appetite. When Casey was clean, he was remorseful and fought hard to get his life back on track. It was a roller-coaster battle that lasted eight long painful years.

It was also during this time that opiod addiction had come to light in the media, and it was finally talked about in many social circles too. Many people were impacted by this opiate crisis, and it gained attention in the media. It was an addiction that did not discriminate, and it will destroy anyone who opens the door to experiment with this type of high. There were journalists who came out and spoke of loved ones that had been affected, and slowly but surely, there it was in the spotlight on national television in living rooms all over the world.

The message is opioid addiction is real and it is killing our loved ones daily, and it does not discriminate by gender, status in society or ethnic group. It was a relief to know that this epidemic of opioid addiction had come to light in the media. There are many people who no longer had to suffer in silence. An injection called Narcan that has the capability of bringing people back to life after an overdose occurs gave some hope to struggling addicts and their families. What a discovery, sobering reality for many. A journalist told a heart-wrenching story of his brother who died from a drug overdose and how that impacted his life and life of his family. Just bringing this to the surface and bringing awareness to this epidemic truly is amazing! The mere education and awareness can change circumstances and impact lives. The one thing that Steve and I agreed upon was that no matter how bad the addiction became and how painful the process, we would always love our son and support him through it even at a distance. Many people were shocked by our resilience and commitment to loving and supporting our son. We never gave up on Casey. We created healthy boundaries along the way, but we never abandoned him or left him feeling hopeless. I often said, "Casey, I love you, and God will carry you when you are weak." I later discovered that Casey held on tight to those words of encouragement in our conversations, and they gave him hope. That was a pearl in my oyster!

After he was released from Wilmington Treatment Center, we took a family trip to the mountains. It was around the time of spring break for most public schools, and we needed this diversion away from the craziness. This uninvited *monster* that controlled every aspect of our lives and destroyed relationships was at least for a time on hold during our trip to the Virginia mountains and Cascade Falls. That was a restful and peaceful trip. We enjoyed being together as a family. It felt like a breath of fresh air and a place that addiction could not touch us!

Returning home was both sad and disappointing because it meant we had to face the reality that our son was still facing a giant, and we had very little control over it. God had to remind me over and over to *let go and let God*. I wanted so desperately to believe that God had Casey under his provision, and he would protect him from this stronghold. However, my motherly instinct was so strong and wanted to fix the problem or pray it away. I had to remind myself that *God* loves him more than me, and he has a purpose for his life. I held onto that promise for dear life and had to constantly repeat that out loud and believe with all the conviction I could muster, that is the truth! Satan told me lies, and some days, in my weakness, I actually believed the lies that led me down a very dark and lonely path; the battle with Satan was not over.

In July of 2015 Casey decided to live with friends and his girlfriend, so we had very little control over his life. One day, he called us and stated he was hurt and needed immediate medical care. Of course, we responded with urgency! He claimed he was playing basketball. We took him to an orthopedic doctor, and they determined from an X-ray that Casey had a very severe break. It was his right leg, and he needed surgery to repair the damage to his tibia. The doctor explained the procedure; it would require several hours to fuse the bone back together using steel rods and bolts. The surgery would repair his broken tibia and allow him to regain full mobility over time. The surgery was costly, and the insurance did not cover all the cost. The surgeon also said Casey's recovery would be long and hard, and he would have to remain still and follow his direct orders for healing to take place over time. The surgeon said Casey would have to take narcotics during the recovery process because he could not manage the pain on his own.

We spoke to the doctor and explained that Casey has a history of addiction and asked if there is another way to manage his pain without narcotics. The doctor said no "because the pain medication was crucial for this type of surgery, and we would need to control how much pain meds were needed." Oh wow! "How in the world could we know his pain levels?" He could lie to us just to get the highest dosage. After all, it was *not* his first rodeo with narcotics. We reluctantly agreed and made sure the narcotics were locked in a safe with the key hidden in our possession. Casey stayed high on narcotics for weeks, and he loved it! His old friend addiction had won again! This time, from a legitimate source and not from the streets but through a prescription from his orthopedic doctor.

Days after his surgery, Casey did something I could not wrap my brain around. He devised a scheme with his girlfriend to get out of the house. I guess, he was climbing the walls and feeling too confined. Without any signs or warnings, he prepared to get to the door on crutches, get in his wheelchair, and escape from the house. I was on the phone at the time and did not notice until he was wheeling himself up the street in his wheelchair. I was shocked and thought to myself I have seen everything now! I followed him and found his girlfriend's father hoisting him into the back of his Jeep. I yelled for him to "stop!" and with conviction, I said to Casey, "If you leave here, do not come back!" "You will not have your narcotics for pain, and I do not care!" He proceeded to slowly get out of the Jeep. I took him back home where he could receive adequate care. Being his caregiver was more than I could handle alone.

As his leg healed, and he received rehab to increase his mobility, I could tell the narcotics he was prescribed was causing him to become dependent again and more impatient and irritated. At his appointments with the surgeon, Casey spoke to the surgeon and told him he needed a refill of his pain meds. I questioned this but allowed it as long as we had it locked up in a safe place. He often complained about the pain, but we stuck to a schedule and did not waver. Within a few weeks, he was healed and ready to return to work. That was a relief! The war on drugs was still in our lives and seemed to find its comfort there. The next few years, passed and Casey lived with his girlfriend in a small house in her bedroom. He was not allowed to live with us as long as addiction was in his life. We had to love him from a distance and pray for his safety during this season.

During the time of separation, Casey was not allowed on our property or in our home. It was during this time that Casey stole an heirloom from his sister's bedroom. He stole a pink sapphire ring that was given to me by my grandmother. It was a cherished heirloom and one of a kind. I gave it to Kelsey on her sixteenth birthday. It was Thanksgiving Day, and we had planned to invite Casey over with the family but soon realized the precious heirloom went missing that very day. The addict mentality used the holidays to try and gain our sympathy and allow him back into our lives. We fell victim to this scheme for years only to be disappointed and hurt all over again. It was a vicious and cruel cycle that controlled us as a family. Many years later, Casey admitted to stealing the ring and pawning it for the gold. That was infuriating to all of us especially Kelsey. Kelsey was so hurt to her core, and she *never* was able to forgive Casey. This was a setback for an already struggling relationship.

On another occasion, somehow Casey was resourceful enough to climb a ladder to break into the upstairs while we were at work. He stole my checkbook to write checks for himself, and his girlfriend forged my signature. I reported both incidents to the authorities only to be told if I pressed charges, both would go to prison for a very long time. They would have multiple felonies on both of their records. I wanted Casey and his girlfriend to suffer the consequences but not in that way. I made a deal with Casey that if he repaid all of the money he tried to steal from me by a deadline, I would not press charges. He lived up to the agreement and was relieved to know he would not go to prison. Both Casey and his girlfriend were codependents at the time and worked as a team to find and secure drugs together to share.

Because of my compassion and mercy, they both dodged a bullet that would impact them for a lifetime.

Another incident where Casey reached his boiling point was when we had set boundaries and he was not allowed on our property. Casey showed up at our house under the influence. He banged on the front door repeatedly, yelling and screaming. We refused to open the door and asked him to leave. Trying to rationalize with anyone under the influence is futile. I picked up the phone and called the police; he was now a trespasser on our property. Tough love was very hard but necessary. He reached his boiling point and charged his hand and arm through the double paned window. The window shattered into a million pieces. He was cut, and the EMS arrived to take care of the self-inflicted wounds. He was removed from our property by the police. Just another reminder of our urgent need for setting boundaries and space between ourselves and addiction. It broke my heart to see Casey injured and hurt, but we had to protect our property. For many weeks and months, the broken glass was a constant reminder of our broken lives.

Every single holiday or birthday was met with bad and embarrassing behavior. It did not matter who was there or how it impacted us. The only thing that seemed to matter was chasing the next opportunity to get high. Steve and I agreed it had left scars so deep that we were barely able to function in real life. We tried to separate the person from the disease, but he seemed to be one and the same most of the time. When I missed Casey, I would pick up the phone to talk to him, but there was no more opportunity to be in the same house together. I decided at that moment that I deserved to reclaim my life and be as happy as possible. I no longer could fight this *monster*, so I turned it over to God and prayed for him from a distance. I knew I had to *let go* and *let God!* I needed to be still and stop trying to solve the problem in my own strength.

I had to give it to Him who is the conqueror of all **(Psalm 46:10)**. This same theme kept me sane in times of utter desperation. The more I let go and allowed *God* to work, the more peace I claimed. This was a pearl in my oyster. Slowly but surely, I was learning what God needed for me to do. That was to give up control of

Casey and let God work in and through Casey's life. Once I made that a consistent permanent practice, I slowly but surely regained my own life back.

Casey had to suffer the consequences of his own bad choices, and as his parents, we had no option but to sit back and let it happen. No more rescuing him from his own destructive behaviors and choices. Even the death threats he would make fell on deaf ears but ripped into my soul and left me weeping for hours. I had to be stronger than this *monster* to survive. Casey later confided in me that that was the turning point for him as well. He saw that we would no longer allow the disease to invade our lives and cause us great pain and suffering.

It was very hard to be strong and consistent and show no emotion, especially for me. This *monster* might win the battle but not the war!

The Path to Forgiveness

Looking from the outside in, one can never understand it. Looking from the inside out, one can never truly explain it. This is how I felt growing up in a family wrapped so tightly around the evil disease of addiction. Addiction was all-encompassing to my family. Every single part of our lives was surrounded and suffocated by the presence of addiction. Like an evil serpent slithering its way into unforeseen circumstances, addiction made its way into our lives. It took away who my brother really was and flipped my family's world upside down.

From the time I was born, my brother Casey and I had a special bond. He took on the role of my "protector" from a young age. He was kind, gentle, and loving as a young boy. I remember my grandparents surprised me with a little red Jeep when I was about five years old. The first thing Casey did was drive me around in that little red Jeep because he was the oldest, and of course, he had to check it out first. At that moment, I did not realize he was serving as my protector and was providing guidance for me in life. Whenever we crossed the street, his hand reached out to hold mine to make sure I got to the other side safely. He taught me things as a young child and found joy in being a big brother.

Life was good for me as a child living in a loving home with supportive and wonderful parents. We spent most of the time making memories together as a family. Summer vacations were spent in Daytona and Naples, Florida, building sandcastles and boogie boarding into the waves with my big brother. Winters were spent sledding in the neighborhood with all of our friends. We had some great times growing up, but sadly, over time, those memories faded away and were replaced with the nightmare that I could not wake up from.

From a young age, my brother always hung around kids who were slightly older than him. To my family and me, we thought this could be good for his friends to serve as somewhat of a mentor for him. Casey was a smart kid; he knew right from wrong and had the same values and morals instilled in him by my parents at a very young age as I did. Yet he chose a much different path from me in life—a path that felt never ending and excruciatingly painful to those who were in his way. I think the tables turned for him when our uncle passed away in 2007. We had already been through some very difficult deaths in the family on my dad's side, and uncle Ron's death particularly felt absolutely gut-wrenching to all of us. One day, he was alive and well; the next he was gone. There was no warning, no medical diagnosis, nothing. Casey was very close to my Uncle Ron. They shared a special bond just like we did as kids. His death hit the entire family very hard. For Casey, it spiraled him down a dark path of destruction.

I would be lying to you if I said it was not painful to write this chapter. However, my hopes are that my story will shed light and hope into someone dealing with this awful addiction. I remember vividly feeling so terrified and lost as I lived through this disease with my brother and my family. None of my friends understood what I was going through. Some of my own family members could not wrap their heads around the capacity of the situation. I felt trapped inside a dark room with no light and no hope. There were days that I lashed out in anger and frustration and days I cried myself to sleep not knowing if my brother would be alive when I woke up. And the worst of them all were the nights I was scared for my life. You see, addiction is a *monster*. It changes the person from the outside in and to the point that you do not even recognize the person standing in front of you. I am not exaggerating when I say I saw the devil in my brother's eyes during the darkest days. The evil was burning through his soul and ripping away every single part of him!

The saying, "You are who you associate with, so choose your friends wisely" is such a true statement. Those who you surround yourself with are likely to influence your life in positive or negative ways. They often influence your decisions, actions, and attitude, and before you know it, you have to choose which gate to enter. Jesus said, **"Enter through the narrow gate. For wide is the gate and broad is the road that leads to destruction, and many enter through it. But small is the gate and narrow the road that leads to life, and only a few find it"** (Matthew 7:13–14 NIV). There was a day when Casey chose the wide gate and never looked back.

The addiction started with smoking marijuana socially with friends and then led into an extreme addiction to alcohol which then led to heroin. Casey said that the high just was not enough anymore. He always needed more, and his body craved ravenously for it. All his thoughts, feelings, and actions were encompassed by the need for the next high. Casey told me that when he woke up in the morning, the first thought that came to his head was, "How am I going to get high today?"

I remember vividly the first time I saw my brother using hard drugs. It was a Saturday morning, and I heard constant snorting coming from his bedroom next door. At this age, I was not oblivious to the evils of the world, but I never thought my own brother would partake. I quickly opened his bedroom door to find him snorting a crushed-up pill on his dresser. The fear in his eyes is something I will never forget. This was the first time anyone in the family had physically seen him using drugs. He begged me to not tell Mom and Dad and assured me it was nothing. Of course, I ran down the stairs to my parents where they were patiently waiting for us to come down for breakfast. With worry and tears in my eyes, I told my parents what I had witnessed. Their initial reaction was disbelief. They were not ready to accept that their own child was an addict. I remember feeling so angry because they did not believe me, but I knew that it would not be long before they did. From that moment, my brother was never the same.

Casey found every way to disguise his addiction. I remember he always took long showers, and when I say long, I mean an hour or so. I was also very suspicious of this. What he was doing behind closed doors in my family's own home was indescribable. We would go out to dinner as a family, but Casey always stayed behind. He used every opportunity he was alone to use drugs. Unfamiliar faces would walk through the doors of our home, and worry began to take over me. I watched my own brother walk down the path of destruction, and I felt hopeless.

Money and materialistic items began to disappear little by little. The addiction took over my brother's life, and in the meantime, my heart was broken as I witnessed it firsthand. At times, I felt like the world was spinning around me nonstop, and I was stuck frozen in the center of it all. It felt as if I was in the eye of a hurricane, but it was a hurricane that lingered on and on. My brother robbed my family not only of money and materialistic items but also of life, joy, and any happiness. The warm and comforting feeling that was once felt in our home quickly faded away. Warmth and comfort turned into sorrow, anger, and discomfort. The home that built me turned into the place that I no longer wanted to enter at the end of the day.

I tried to hide my emotions for a while, but it never worked. My friends, family members, and even teachers started seeing a change in me. The sweet smiles and bright eyes turned into frowns and hopeless eyes. I was scared; I was worried, and I was unhappy because of the *monster* of addiction that walked into our home.

One day I'll never forget is April 15, 2010, which just so happened to be my fourteenth birthday. Just like any other school day, I got dressed and ready and jumped in the car to be dropped off in the carpool line that morning. I was in eighth grade at the time. Little did I know what would happen on this day and the events that would be to come. The bell rang at 3:25 p.m. as usual, and I headed to the front of the school where my mom would be waiting in the carpool line to pick me up from school. My mom was a teacher at the high school my brother attended, which just so happened to be right down the street from my middle school. I remember waiting outside the front of the school talking with friends waiting for my mom to arrive, but she was running later than usual on this day. I thought maybe she got caught up in a meeting at work or was just running a little behind. As time passed by, I realized I was one of the last kids waiting for their parents in front of that middle school and began to worry. Moments later, my mom pulled up, but today, I wasn't greeted with a friendly smile and "Hey, honey, how was your day?" Instead, I was greeted with a face of disappointment and eyes red and swollen from the tears she had shed. Immediately, I knew something was wrong, and the first thing that came out of my mouth was, "What did Casey do now?" Now I know that sounds harsh, but at this point, my brother was a wild card. We never knew what was coming next other than it more than likely wasn't going to be good.

I remember my mom turning to look at me, and all I could see was pure disappointment and defeat in her eyes. The only thing that came out of her mouth was, "Today has not been a good day sweetie, I'm sorry." I've always had a pretty good intuition and knew something was seriously wrong. I had a gut-wrenching feeling that my brother had been arrested, and to my dismay, I was correct. My mom tried to hide it with it being my birthday, but as soon as the words came out of my mouth, she confirmed what my gut was telling me. To say the least, that was a not so happy birthday for me. We ended up spending the night bailing my brother out of jail instead of blowing out candles and making birthday wishes.

As the years went on, things continued to get worse. My brother's addiction caused a rift in our family. My parents' relationship suffered, and I was caught in the middle of it all, once again. There were several times I had wished I could just run away from it all. But I knew I couldn't abandon my family during the most difficult time. The one thing that kept me going was my faith. No matter how difficult things got, I knew the Lord was by my side through it all. His steadfast love and guidance was the glue that held me together during those years.

Now as an adult, I realize just how much my brother's addiction impacted me. I wish I could tell you that today things are great, and Casey and I have a strong, loving relationship, but that wouldn't be the truth. After I graduated from college, I took the first opportunity to move away from my hometown to start a new life for myself. Mainly because I was tired of living under the shadow of my brother and his choices but also because I knew if I did not spread my wings, I would never know what it truly feels like to be free—free from constant worry, anger, and resentment. I needed to begin my life because for so long, it felt as if I was never going to get out of that dark hole. Addiction is all-consuming for all parties involved. Watching someone you love and care about so much change into someone you don't even recognize when they are standing right in front of you is traumatic.

To be honest, my brother and I do not have a good relationship or any relationship at this point. It's difficult to say, but the one feeling that I always come back to is resentment. There are things that have happened in the past that have caused me to have hard feelings and feel bitter toward my own brother. I am hopeful that as time goes on and I heal from the past, we will have a great relationship like we once did as little kids riding around in that little red jeep.

Today, I have a slightly different view as I look through the rearview mirror. Because I was the youngest in the family who witnessed and lived through everything, I am a strong, resilient, and a faithful woman today. My life certainly was not easy when I grew up; however, my life then shaped me to be who I am today. I hope that whoever is reading this is comforted knowing that it's okay for things not to be okay. We all go through hardships in life and experience things that others may not understand. But I am here to tell you, you are not alone. Give yourself space and grace to not forget your past but to forgive. Remember this verse when you are going through a difficult time in life: **Jeremiah 29:11 says, "For I know the plans I have for you, declares the Lord plans to prosper you and not to harm you, plans to give you a hope and a future."** On the hardest of days, this verse carried me through.

Cruising into the Twenties and Crashing

This spiral of addiction continued into Casey's twenties. On his twenty-first birthday, we decided to take our first cruise to celebrate Kelsey's graduation and our 25th wedding anniversary, and his milestone birthday of turning twenty-one years of age. Casey was on probation at the time; therefore, we had to get special permission to take him out of the country from the court system. It was apparent that the ugliness of addiction would follow us on this beautiful trip and try to destroy any happiness we tried to have. This time, the *monster was alcohol*. He drank every day and found himself making a fool of himself. His behavior was shocking and unacceptable. Why couldn't Casey just, this one time, allow us to enjoy this cruise and make lasting memories together as a family?

Casey was found at the bar drinking until late into the night and all hours of the morning. He had very little desire to be with family or enjoy the trip without alcohol. The excursions on the islands in the Western Caribbean were about the only refuge away from the relentless drinking. Casey was an angry drunk, and he was not pleasant to be around. Casey was so drunk the morning we docked to return home that he was almost left on the boat as other passengers were filing out of the boat. What a trip to remember!

He slept all the way back home that day. It was a sobering reminder of what alcohol and drugs could do to ruin his life. No substance seemed to be off-limits. After returning home, Casey's new vice to wrestle with was alcohol. This was a more popular substance that was generally accepted by the majority of people; however, with

Casey's reckless history of substance abuse, it was just yet another *monster* to fight along his path. Alcohol, especially liquor, turned Casey into a very angry person that looked like a demon at times. He could not just drink in moderation; he had to finish whatever he started, whether it was a fifth of liquor or a twelve pack of beer. It did not matter. The alcohol controlled his actions and circumstances. During this turbulent time, we refused to allow him to drive, so he relied on others for transportation. His buddies picked him up, and he stayed away for days. When he did happen to stumble home, he was not welcome, and the doors to our home were locked and secured for our own safety. At times, he was violent and dangerous. We conveniently left the hammock out or the lounge on the patio available with a blanket to cover himself. He knew not to be expected to sleep in his warm cozy bed in that condition. In the nearby bushes, we would find particles of vomit where he released the alcohol from the night before. It was disgusting!

His reckless behavior could not be ignored. He stashed his evidence of beer cans, liquor bottles, etc. in all of the secret places of our home. He could not deny that alcohol was just another substance that had a tight grip on him. I could not have any alcohol in the house for myself nor could Steve enjoy an occasional beer or mixed drink. It was too risky to have it in the house around him. I can remember when Steve bought a huge chain that he wrapped around the refrigerator just to keep Casey away from any alcohol.

During this time, Casey was also enrolled at a local community college where he took classes to get a degree in computer science. He had completed some of his classes but had some left to officially get a degree. The struggle to study and absorb the information and apply it was a struggle because Casey was also employed part-time by a landscaping company. Imagine adding alcohol to that!

As I look back, I see that he may have cruised into his twenties, but he crashed hard. He struggled to make it in life because of his addiction. While most of his high school classmates succeeded with education and jobs, Casey let the *monster* have control of his life. Casey remained a pearl in my oyster, but I had to look hard and remove the sand and grit to find a little view of it. I continued to pray knowing that God could turn his life around if Casey would surrender.

When Casey drank excessively, he got angry and lashed out physically and verbally. On two separate occasions, he broke his hand, hitting a wall. On another occasion, in an angry rage, he hit our metal mailbox; that dent is still there as a reminder of his volatile temper. We spent many hours in consultation and meetings with therapists and psychiatrists to determine the cause of his anger. Casey stayed away from us most of the time during this season of abusing alcohol. The *monster* had a tight grip on him and would not let go. On one cold wintery night, we got a dreaded call in the middle of the night that a car was located on the beltline with the driver and passenger still in the car in the median. The officer arrived to find two very drunk individuals. When the officer opened the door, both fell out on the cold hard ground. The officer said no one was hurt, luckily, and they made the right decision to pull over. We were called to pick Casey up, and the driver was arrested. On another occasion, we were startled by a phone call from a neighbor in the community who had witnessed an accident. We arrived on the scene to find Casey was under the influence of drugs and alcohol. He fell asleep behind the wheel and ran into the ditch. Luckily, he was not injured, but the truck was totaled. So thankful it was not a fatal accident or accident that involved another car. We had to contact the police and turn him in. It started snowing that night, and I looked up to the heavens for answers to this situation. We waited with Casey until the police arrived. He was like a caged animal trying to defend himself and get out of a cage. He knew, when the blue lights came down the road, what the outcome would be for him. He was arrested and charged with DWI. Casey could not write a statement for the records; he was too disoriented and troubled. I had a quilt wrapped around him to keep him warm for the ride to the police station, where he would stay the night. That was one of the hardest days of my life. Did Casey have a death wish, or was he just careless and reckless? The court date was set, and here we go again. This was an all too familiar place, and pretty soon, the judge would know him by name as a repeat offender.

This court date was one I will never forget because of the kindness shown to me by a stranger. I was sitting waiting for his case to be called, and the lady next to me noticed I was reading a bible study. She politely asked if I am a Christian, and I replied, "Yes, I am, but lately, my faith is dim." She asked if the young man in the front row was my son, and I replied, "Yes."

She said to me with kindness and concern, "Casey will be alright if he will just turn toward Jesus and follow him." After his case was heard, she asked if she could pray over us. I was shocked but willing. We held hands and prayed. Others even joined in the prayer circle. It was a powerful moment in time that I needed. It was as if Jesus sent an angel to me that day. I did not catch her name. She smiled and walked away into the distance. That was the encouragement I needed at that exact moment, so I know it was not just a coincidence. Casey's record was piling up, and he was a frequent flier in the courtroom. I prayed for Jesus to take this stronghold away so Casey could lead a normal life without the monster, *alcohol,* on his back. A few years later, my prayer was answered as God, in his infinite mercy and grace, took the need for alcohol away from him. I cannot recall the exact moment or time, but he turned away from this *monster* and has not had any problems since. Casey's favorite saying is, "Failure is the best teacher." He learned from his failures finally and made a conscious decision to not continue down that path. His dad and I both were very grateful that Casey made that decision on his own to stop drinking and clear his name and record.

A Father's Love

To understand my journey with my son's addiction, I have to reflect on the history of my family and the dynamics of our relationships. I grew up as the youngest boy of three. My father and mother worked hard to provide for us. My dad did hard manual labor and worked with his hands in marble and stone. My mother worked for the State of North Carolina in many different roles. She was the protector and provider of all things we needed. We lived a modest lifestyle and loved each other.

My dad was rough around the edges and rarely home. He mainly worked out of town. My dad loved his alcohol and would drink mostly on weekends to relax and unwind. David was the brother I was the closest to when we grew up. We shared bunkbeds; I slept on the bottom, and he slept on the top. We lived in a small but adequate split-level house. David would wait until I just dozed off to sleep, and he would hang down from his bunk like a limp dead man with his eyes rolling back in his head. I was terrified as a young boy. He would laugh out loud, and I would get so angry. I looked up to and admired David. I can remember back in the 1970s when peace and love were celebrated and women's rights: long hair hippies and rock and roll. David had a Chevy van that he bought and parked outside on the street. He took an automotive class in high school, and he was even in a club that worked on engines and the interior. It was an exclusive club. The van was spray-painted bright orange on the outside and decked out on the inside. He rebuilt the engine, and it was one of the fastest on the block. It had a bed and many conveniences that most small houses have. David also drove a school bus in high school and parked it in front of the house. David was very smart and talented. It is kind of easy to see why I admired my brother.

After high school, he decided to attend North Carolina State University. He was very proud to be a member of the pack and wore the red and white emblem proudly. He pursued a degree in political science and hoped to get his license to be an attorney. Our uncle is a family attorney, and David wanted to walk in his footsteps to become an attorney. In the summer, David spent time with Uncle Howard, and they enjoyed a smoke and drink together. I can remember playing pool with Dad and David at the Cary Tavern. I have good memories of those days and bonding over beers and pool games. Dad and David were top competitors, and they often put a wager on their games. One night after work, Dad went out to play pool and had one too many beers. He started his drive home, and not long after, I received my first ever phone call from the police. My dad was arrested for his first and only DWI. I was the son who bailed him out of jail and brought him home that night. That night became one I will never forget.

David became the proud owner of a downtown local bar.

I came home from East Carolina University on weekends; I worked the pool table area on occasions. I was proud of his accomplishment; however, I was not thrilled that his college goals and future plans to get a degree in political science became less important and was replaced with making money and being popular. David spent six years trying to take courses at North Carolina State while juggling the business. It became too much! My brother got involved with shady characters and soon started drinking after hours and doing cocaine. He took long road trips to distant places to chase the next high. David's nights were spent drinking heavily, doing drugs, and playing pool with locals. David spent his days sleeping off hangovers and drug use, and he spent his nights working in the bar. I cannot recall seeing David much during those days. Occasionally, he took a road trip to ECU to show me the ropes and how to party as a rookie college student. I loved those weekends with my brother. He told stories, and it felt just like old times. He would say things like, "Shit happens," and "Hair don't grow on rock, boy," as he referred to his body and facial hair. My buddies and I would laugh, and we would enjoy those times. I was just a rookie learning the ropes of the college experience.

After I graduated from ECU I returned to my hometown and rented my first house with my best buddy Michael. We had our very own bachelor pad in the form of a one hundred-year-old white colonial house. The owner was a sweet old lady well-known within the Garner community. She said, "I never rented to two young boys before, but you two seem very nice and clean." The two-story tin roof house had two bedrooms and two baths, a huge kitchen, and family room. There were pecan trees outside and a big backyard.

Soon after, David and I decided to buy a boat together in 1985. I remember cleaning it up one summer day and sitting in it telling stories of the past and drinking beers together. David and I were so proud of our purchase, and we got a bumper sticker to put on it to seal the deal and partnership. I was raised to keep things clean and take care of things so this boat would be no exception. I took it out on the lake, came back, and cleaned it up. It never was trashy or dirty. However, David just saw it as recreation and conversation piece for bragging rights with his buddies. He did not have the same philosophy as me, and that caused some friction at times. I loved my brother, but sometimes, his excessive drinking and old stories were annoying and embarrassing. My admiration for him grew dimmer, and I knew I wanted a better life than just bragging rights.

I interviewed and accepted a job with the State of North Carolina in 1985, and shortly after that, I married Cathy on August 20, 1988. Cathy knew my family, and we dated over a span of about seven years. David moved to Cary, and we were only miles apart, but in my heart, it was much farther. Our relationship changed. I made a life with Cathy, and a few years later, our family grew. Casey and Kelsey changed our lives and priorities. Unfortunately, my brother David remained stuck in the past. He still drank excessively and continued to do drugs. His business failed, and he lost ownership. He never completed the college degree he had once made a goal to achieve. Unfinished goals and a life of addiction are all that remained, broken pieces of a life that could have been great. He never married, so he died alone. It was a terrible death in April of 2003 which was six months after my mother passed away. He was alone with a gun pointed at his head. He found himself faced with nothing else to live for. He tried to get help in rehabs and treatment centers to no avail. He always fell back into old habits. He took his own life and left behind family with broken pieces of his life that has never made sense.

My brother's death was shocking, and it is one day I will never forget. My dear sweet mother had passed away October of 2002 from cancer, and David just could not stand the grief and pain of losing the one person who stayed connected during the dark days of addiction. I was devastated and had such remorse that hurt me to my core. For months and years prior to his death, I did not maintain contact. However, I wish I was there for him as he battled addiction and the dark, evil days that lurked around him and would not let him live the life he wanted. But in the end, he was too weak and too ashamed to fight the *monster* anymore. I remember he called Kelsey on her birthday a few days prior to his death and spoke to her. David never really knew my children and was not involved in their lives for reasons I never understood. But that day, he reached out for the first time to talk to her as her uncle she never met. Shortly after, he took his own life.

Questions surround me like a cycle of destruction and desperation. What should I have done to help save his life? Could I have made a difference in some way? Why did I not pursue him? David became invisible to me and the family toward the end. Was his death premeditated? Had he been planning his own exit from this earth? Had he calculated all of the details and carefully and methodically planned his own suicide? I wish I could have had one last communication with him. I had many questions and no answers. My mother was the only one who understood David and the struggles he faced as an addict. She was the only one with knowledge that he did pursue interventions for addictions. The answers are now buried with her in that tomb where she lay. The viewing of David's body before the burial was more than I could bare. As I stood over his lifeless body, I promised myself if I had a boy one day and he became involved with drugs or alcohol, I would do everything in my human power to help my son through this so the outcome would *not* be the same. The generational curse that took my brother's life too soon would not take a son of mine. The shame, hurt, and grief was unbearable. My father, who was diagnosed with colon cancer, had to be told of the tragedy, and I had to be the one to tell him. That reality shook me to my core.

When David died, it left just dad, Ron, and his son Parker and me to carry on the Ennis name. My oldest brother Ron passed away unexpectedly from a heart attack in December of 2007. Within a period of several years, my entire family was erased from the earth. I have just the memories I keep close to my heart, and I treasure the time I spent with them. I could not fully understand or justify why God would take my entire family away from me.

When I was married and started my own family, it was a relief and blessing for me. I held on tight to the relationships with great resolve and appreciation for life. When my one and only son was in the fight for his life with a similar *monster* as my brother David, I had to do everything in my power to keep him alive and never ever give up on him no matter the circumstances or how bad things got. My personal resolve and conviction come from the past mistakes I made. The outcome for my son would be different, and as his father, I was determined to fight for him and the life I envisioned for Casey.

I noticed similarities in my brother and Casey as he was growing up into a young man. Casey is very tall and slender like David. His facial structure and features are almost identical. David had a false sense of pride and confidence in himself at times, and so did Casey. Both David and Casey loved the attention of the ladies. They presented themselves as handsome and charming young men. Both very intelligent however made bad choices in life. Their goals were not fully accomplished and dreams put on hold. It is crystal clear that David and Casey share the same DNA and similar traits. But what I do not want them to share is the end of their story. David's journey through life ended in sadness and tragedy. If I had just done things differently and supported and loved him through addiction, maybe the outcome for him might have been different. I made a conscious decision to love Casey unconditionally the day he was born and to fight for his life when the battle was on. Our relationship as father and son had changed drastically during those teenage years. Casey became disrespectful and saw my guidance as an intrusion and attempt to control him. Our calm discussions became power struggles and loud irrational bouts of tempers and verbal attacks. Many of these moments turned into physical wrestling matches. I am not an emotional person, so my disappointment was turned inward and manifested itself in different ways. I coped by working long hours and talked to anyone who would listen. My role had changed to the rescuer and protector from the monster. During those days, I fought hard for my son's freedom from addiction, and I slept very little. My resolve and perseverance paid off in the long run because our relationship today is much healthier. A father's love for his son is greater than any *monster,* and it turns out that my instincts were right, which led to a turning point along our journey.

Casey's Reflections and Turning Point

My drug use and abuse has led me to do a lot of self-reflection. When I was caught up in the vicious cycle of use, abuse, self-medicate, and use again, I did not think about those that were affected by my bad choices and behaviors. I was not concerned with the social, emotional, or personal suffering my addiction had caused. It was only when I was detoxed and thinking rational that I accepted responsibility for my actions and behaviors. When I was sober and not using drugs, I felt an overwhelming sense of shame, regret, and remorse. It was as if I had to start all over again building relationships and building trust with anyone and everyone I had hurt or offended in some way. Most of my relationships were toxic when I was using drugs.

I loved my family, and they were about the only healthy relationship I could count on. I would ask myself, "How could they possibly love me and trust me again?" I have hurt them over and over. However, no matter what I did and no matter the distance, I was always forgiven by my parents. Their unconditional love and tough love at times kept me striving to do better and be better. When I was away from home, I longed for their love and conversation. When I spoke to either of them or Kelsey, I felt a sense of relief and genuine happiness and joy. I felt a sense of security and safeness that I did not feel anywhere else. As my addiction grew and continued, Mom and Dad received guidance and advice from the professionals, and as a result, they would not allow me to stay in their home, allow my addiction to infiltrate their lives, or allow this situation to cause them more pain (though I realize now that they were still emotionally hurting even though they distanced me from them). My house was no longer a revolving door that opened and closed on my selfish command.

During the times of sobriety, I reflected a lot on forgiveness. I prayed to God for forgiveness. I knew enough about the Bible that the teachings were clear. **God will forgive those who come to confess their sins and he will hear their prayers and forgive them no matter the offense or the sin (1 John 1:9).** Any sin is the same in God's eyes, and there is no unforgivable sin according to the Bible. I knew God would forgive me. Though I knew this, I wondered how I could possibly forgive myself for all the pain and suffering I had caused. In addition, I wondered how family, friends, and others could ever forgive me. Did I deserve their forgiveness? I learned the hard way that this is a process, and it may take many years to achieve this. Even to this day, I really struggle with forgiving myself for all the hurt and pain I have caused throughout the years. I cannot find the words to express how I felt then, and I remember well how I struggled with initiating this. Through time, counseling, therapy, and prayers, I am slowly learning to forgive myself. My church family has been a huge support system for me, and I appreciate all of their kindness, compassion, and accountability. Slowly but surely, God is showing me how to forgive myself and how to have patience with others who may not be as forgiving.

The day I was baptized on that campus was the beginning of a fresh start in life. **I have to accept that I am not perfect, and I have fallen short of God's plan for me (Romans 3:23).** I am a work in progress, and I must be patient and accept any regression or bad choices I might make in the future. My whole life has been a series of steps moving forward and then steps back; it is such a frustrating place to be in life. My greatest fear is to be forty years old and not have made any progress in life. I remain in a rut that has caused me great frustration. I never ever want to go back to the life of an addict; it is no way to live. There are still so many goals and things I want to achieve in life, and I refuse to go backward. As long as I have a mustard seed of faith and hope, I know I will eventually forgive myself and move forward instead of backward because **Jesus said faith moves "mountains" (Matthew 17:20).**

I have so many regrets in life. I regret the way I treated my little sister Kelsey. She deserved to have a loving big brother to grow up with. Instead, she got a big brother that did not treat her fairly, made fun of her, and was physically and emotionally abused by me. I can remember her asking me if she could hang out with my friends. My response was an angry and hurtful, "No! Go away!" I stole from her own bedroom. At times, I threatened her and made her be fearful for her own life. The things I said to her are, honestly, unforgivable. I did not attend important events in her life including her own college graduation, most of her birthdays, and other special occasions that a big brother should have supported her through. Our relationship has been battered, bruised, and scared in ways that I have no idea how to begin to repair the damage I have caused.

A major regret is not walking across the stage of my own high school graduation; instead, my diploma was mailed to me. That was a blow to my parents and my poor choices that took the day of joy away from them. The reality of my poor choices had consequences that affected everyone in my life.

Another regret is not finishing my degree in computer science. I only have a few hours of instruction and classes left to meet this goal, but that has been sidelined for various reasons. Now I am in a job that does bring me great fulfillment and joy, and it pays the bills. It provides a paycheck and something I can see myself doing for the rest of my life.

The list of regrets is endless, but I must tackle one at a time and not allow my anxiety to get the best of me. Now that I do not mask my true feelings and emotions with drugs, I have to cope with anxiety in different ways. I am learning to communicate my feelings and emotions and to do this in a way that is healthy and not out of anger and frustration.

The days of Casey lashing out in anger are behind me now. I am proud of the progress I have made in this area, but I still have a long way to go.

Yet another regret I am most upset and have a hard time forgiving myself for is the day my grandmother's car was wrecked and totaled the very first day I received it. I was under the influence of a drug and ran off the road near my home. I had a very serious seizure behind the wheel and could not control what was happening. I called my parents and told them the tire blew out on the white Oldsmobile, but that was only the half of the truth. My parents arrived to find a wrecked and totaled car. My sweet grandma wanted me to have this car after she passed away. She had no idea it would be a wrecked piece of metal in my hands. Prior to this, I had wrecked several cars, and this was the last chance to have transportation. We never told grandmother about her car; it would have surely broken her heart. She was very sick and suffering from liver disease, dementia, and strokes. This news would have surely sent her over the edge, and who knows how she would have taken it.

I think my biggest regret is just not listening to my parents at a young age. I know my life could have been much different had I taken the time to listen to their wisdom and advice. I was influenced by a voice of the enemy instead of the voice of God. I thought my parents were trying to control me, and I was very defiant while I listened to the wrong voice. The voice of reason was overshadowed by another voice that led me down the wrong path. With this, the challenges and struggles I endured were all a part of God's plan for me to depend on him and trust him. The scripture says, **"Do not lean on your own understanding" (Proverbs 3:5)**. In the valleys, I was forced to look toward the light and pray for help and guidance.

I have learned that God is the captain of my life, and I need to trust in him and his plan for my life. **Psalm 46:1 says that God is our shelter and source of strength, and that in times of trouble, he will protect those who trust him.** It has taken me a long time to truly embrace this lesson. I am a sinner saved by grace and thankful for his provision and protection over my life.

New Hope

In September 2017, before the passing of my beloved grandmother, I had something wonderful and unexpected happen in my life. God had spared my life many times and rescued me from the grips of addiction, and I was grateful. At any given time, my Heavenly Father could have taken my life and allowed my own poor choices to be the end of my story. Instead, God chose to use my life experiences to touch others in a powerful way and be a testament to those struggling with addiction. God would, of course, be glorified through it.

I was invited to attend the New Hope Church in Garner by a friend. I knew the friend from previous churches and youth events. I was still struggling with addiction behaviors, but I was accepted as Casey Ennis by this friend and the church. I came as a sinner with all my emotional baggage and tragic past experiences. I was accepted, and I felt a warm welcome from sinners, not saints. After getting involved with the church, I became involved with an organization where I would find and feel my worth. World Changers were those volunteers that offered their time to serve the church and our God. I began to serve as a first contact volunteer with the group, and I seemed to fit right in with many of those who served the church. My role was to help people park their cars and greet them in the parking lot. I worshipped with a diverse group of people that I now call my friends. After a while, I could relate to the senior pastor's testimony, and scripture finally started making sense, and the gospel became relevant to me. I had so many questions about the history of the Bible. This pastor is one I could relate with and understand. His story was very similar to mine in the beginning, and he had come a long way in a better direction. He once suffered from substance abuse and addiction, and he overcame it with God's mercy and grace. Because I knew he traveled down a similar road as I, a connection was made that helped to change my life.

The pastor had a vision of creating a church where anyone and everyone would be welcome to learn about the love of Jesus through the gospel. In time, he became a lead pastor of many campuses. He wrote and published his own book of his own testimony. He was not ashamed or embarrassed about his past. I could finally be in a church and in the fellowship with other believers without being judged or shunned because of my past. I could share my own testimony. After all, the church is for sinners, not saints. The freedom to worship with other believers in a nonjudgmental setting was such a blessing. I am so grateful to the New Hope Church family for giving me hope in a very dark period of my life.

On Sunday, September 24, 2017, I made one of the most important decisions of my life. There was a baptism out front at New Hope Church in Garner, and people were lined up to go into the waters of baptism and profess their faith in God for the first time or rededicate their lives to Christ. There was no appointment necessary or any formalities. It was an invitation to "come as you are" with an open mind and heart to receive Jesus into your lives. One by one, people walked up to make that commitment. My girlfriend and I stepped up in the line, and on that much unexpected day, we rededicated our lives to serve our Lord and Savior. What a glorious day! Years prior to this in February of 2003, I made the same decision but as a younger child.

However, September 24, 2017 was different from my experience in 2003. This time, the baptism was real, and it was powerful with a true commitment for life change as an adult.

As a young adult who experienced everything evil and dark, I was emotionally spent. I was in the lowest of the valleys and even faced death. I had wrestled with the *monsters* (*demons*), but God fought my battles of addiction and won the victory. I was so confident and knew beyond a shadow of a doubt this was the right decision and the right timing to make Jesus Christ my Lord and Savior. I was confident of this decision and had much joy! The campus pastor did the honors of performing baptisms while families and others were witnesses to the transformations that took place right before their eyes. I was given a photo and certificate that I proudly have displayed in my home to remind me of that joyful occasion. I am born again as a new Christian; I have washed away the old self and become a new being through the blood of Jesus. When I made this decision, I knew my life would not suddenly become easier, but I did know—and still know—that My God will be my protector, and he will not leave nor forsake me in times of trouble. This is a promise that I could believe and hold fast to as my journey through life continues.

To further my growth as a new Christian, I signed up for a group called Rooted with my girlfriend. We were part of a bible study we committed to for ten weeks. I learned some valuable lessons and was actively engaged in meaningful conversations that helped me to have a deeper understanding.

The important decision I had made was to follow Jesus through this journey called life. I could understand the Bible study as I read the lessons with Cassandra, and we learned the content together. I opened up about my strongholds and things I had been ashamed and embarrassed to share with others. The participants in the group accepted me, and they did not shun me because of my past. They did not judge me because of my past, and that meant a lot to me. I was once and for all seen as a child of the most high God and loved by him. I learned to pray and talk to God as a broken sinner. This group of people had their own baggage and testimonies to share. There was a bond that was formed between us that was refreshing and very powerful.

I learned that the enemy is a *liar*, and he wants to destroy my life and my dreams of being someone and having a purpose **(John 8:44)**. I listened to the wrong voice for years that whispered things like "You are worthless." "You are not loved," and "You will never amount to anything." But my God speaks the truth through his Word, the gospel. God is more powerful, and he can overcome any sin or obstacle that I encounter. My role is to have faith and believe that God is in control because he wants me to have a full and productive life.

One of the biggest influences in my life at this time was my Grandmother Brannon. A godly woman shared her wisdom with me and stories that will impact me for a lifetime. I lovingly referred to her as my granny.

A Grandmother's Love

This is a turning point in the story with a shift to present Casey's special firsthand experience and his points of view. His words share the reality of what we faced and how a very special person influenced him to turn his life around. These are the words from Casey.

*****

You see, I was able to overcome the *monster*, and it was because I had people who cared about me, prayed for me, and invested their energies to help me. My grandma is one of those important people. She was a pearl in my oyster.

My Grandma Brannon was such a huge influence in my life. She was there for my birth, and she was a constant source of love and security for me. When I was born, Grandma Brannon wrote a poem entitled "My Casey Boy," and in it, she referred to me as the pearl in her oyster. It is so special to me that I still have it hanging on my wall, and obviously, its special to my whole family as the title of this book suggests. I never realized what a gifted writer she was until I matured.

For every birthday, she would write a personal card with a handwritten note of encouragement. I kept every one of her cards to me in two boxes: one in my heart and the other is the physical box. I loved her with all my heart and soul and felt so blessed to have her in my life. During the dark days of addiction, she was my prayer warrior. She would rise every morning to pray for me and often over me. She sat at the kitchen table with her Bible open while she also watched the birds through the window. I remember that she and my grandfather would pray over me and on my behalf. They believed in the power of prayer, and they never gave up on it.

On the rare occasion I could spend time with her, my grandma would talk to me with love and compassion but also with a sternness that caught my attention. Her words and advice were always taken seriously as I respected her wisdom. Very few people had the courage to speak the truth and show tough love to me through my addiction with the *monster*. My grandma and sister Kelsey were the only ones who made me accountable and forced me to tell the truth and speak the truth no matter what the consequence. When my grandma spoke, I listened and heeded her warnings. She spoke to me about God's love for me and his plan for my life. She quoted scriptures like, **"I know the plans I have for you declares the Lord, plans to prosper you and not harm you, plans to give you a hope and a future" from Jeremiah 29:11.** She made the scripture relevant to my circumstances, and she always showed her love and concern for my well-being. She never passed judgment or fussed at me. However, just a look or a few words from her would get my attention. I would always show her respect in her home or anytime I was fortunate enough to spend time with her.

I always felt protected and loved so much at my grandma's home. It was a peaceful setting to just relax and feel safe. I could feel the Holy Spirit there among the tall trees and whispering creek that ran along the bank. When I was a kid, I really enjoyed exploring in the woods, looking for fish and tadpoles. I would take my shoes off and wade in the creek. One summer, my grandparents built a tree house in the woods, and I loved to go up there with my little sister and pretend it was a secret fort. We enjoyed having our own space to call our own. We had chairs and a table to eat on, and we even decorated the walls. Those days spent at our grandparents were very special to me, and I loved the memories that were created there.

As I got older and had my own job and other social adventures, my grandma would call me and ask me to come over to do some yard work for her. She would always offer to pay me, and she always made sure that I ate some food and sat down at the table for conversation. This was not a suggestion. I enjoyed those days and never realized how much I would miss them when she was gone. I think it was her way of seeing how I was doing and forcing me to spend time with her. I never ever regretted those quiet and peaceful times I spent with her. She had a peaceful spirit about her that no one else in my life had at the time. She could calm my mind and spirit with just a hug, smile, or warm pot of soup. I loved her vegetable soup, and she always had it piping hot. It was sometimes the only meal I had for days during my days of addiction. My grandmother also made homemade strawberry preserves. They were delicious, and she always gave me a jar to take with me before leaving. However, when I gave the *monster* room in my life, I didn't have an appetite for her good food. The drugs suppressed my appetite, which was a harsh reality of my addiction.

I remember a conversation we shared that I will never forget. It was the day a switch was flipped, and I realized that with God's help and guidance, I could beat the addiction with the *monster*, and I could live a normal life. It was the day I felt a sense of peace knowing that I would be okay, and I never ever had to live in the shadow of addiction ever again.

My grandma helped me to see that addiction is a disease that did not define me nor did it have the power over my life. God is in control of my life. God did not allow me to die the multiple times I put my own life in jeopardy because of my poor choices. If he wanted me dead, I would not be here today.

My grandma was very wise, and she knew exactly what I needed to hear and when I needed to hear it. It was like she could read my thoughts. She shared with me hardships in her own personal life. She was an accomplished business owner and well-known member of the community. She loved her church and the church community. She served in the children's ministry for years, and she taught bible studies. She wanted the lost to be found and know the love of Jesus. That was her mission in life, and she achieved that in her lifetime. She was an encourager to everyone she met. She was a woman of God and a shining light for many who knew her. Her legacy will live on in my heart forever.

Toward the end of her life, she shared a time that she wanted to give up and take her own life. She had been rejected and betrayed by someone she loved deeply. She had carried this burden for a long time, like Jesus carried that old wooden cross to Calvary. She was scared and hopeless at the time. She devised a plan to take her life, but someone significant in her life, her son Craig, found her and stopped her from doing it. When no one was home, she walked a mile or so to the back of the property, through the crunching leaves, with thoughts of ending it all.

Grandma did not have a backup plan if it failed to work, so she prayed that it would. She got to the open area in the woods and started to cry out to God in desperation. Little did she know her son Craig had skipped school that day and came home. He was not supposed to be at home; it was a weekday, and that was why she planned it for that day.

My heart sank and tears welled up in my eyes when she told me this story. How could this strong woman of God think like that! Who would cause such pain that made her feel hopeless like her life did not matter! Then and there as she told me her story, I made a promise to myself and her that I would never get to that point in desperation, and I would tell someone or call out to God because he would show me a way out of my misery. That was a turning point that I will never forget. She shared her whole heart with me that day and had the courage to speak the truth. I have such respect, love, and admiration for her. She left an imprint in my heart that I will carry forever!

She said to me that humans make mistakes, and they hurt us in ways that scar us for life, but God is everlasting, and he loves us no matter what. His love endures forever! If my grandmother had been successful that day and took her own life, I would have missed out on so many wise lessons and great family times. I was not even born when that happened, and if she had been successful, I would have only known her from photos and through others' memories of her. God knew that she would be saved that day because he had so many more plans for her life. She showed such courage that day and made a decision that affected the whole family. She chose *life* even in the most difficult and dire situations.

The poem Grandma wrote the day of my birth is a legacy she left for me to cherish and share with others. She was a woman of God with many talents, and I feel so blessed to have been her grandchild. The lessons she taught me will live in my heart and mind forever! Her life and legacy will not be forgotten, and I look forward to being reunited with her in heaven one day.

This book is a loving tribute to her and her memory. She would be so proud to see how I am doing now. She would give me a great big hug and say, "I knew you could beat this with Jesus Christ on your side." I often feel her influence and presence especially if I am in a stressful place and need advice or support.

Grandma is responsible for the place where we used to live with my girlfriend Cassandra. It is just a few miles from where she used to call home. My mother went to the graveside one day when we were homeless living in a hotel, and she prayed for shelter for us. Within a few hours, God led her to this place I once called home. It was a gift from heaven that I cannot deny. Grandma's final resting place is only a few miles away, and I go there sometimes to talk to her and share stories. I know her physical body is not in that tomb, but it does my heart good to know I am keeping memories of her and her goodness alive. She is partly responsible for the career I chose for myself in landscaping. She loved her plants, flowers, and God's nature. She helped me to see the beauty in the earth God created, to take care of it, and to nurture so that we can enjoy it. I take great pride in my work, and I love to see nature come together and create a beautiful tapestry for others to enjoy.

Grandma taught me to take pride in my work and to do quality work for others to enjoy. That is a valuable lesson that I hold near and dear to my heart. God has blessed my efforts in the field of landscaping, and that effort has also proven to be a blessing in many ways. On the small property we rent, I planted bushes and flowers to enhance the property and make it look more like home to us. I know my grandmother is smiling down on us as we continue to care for God's creation of plants and flowers. Her legacy lives in me; Grandma is still a prized pearl. Our conversations led me to make the next logical step along this journey.

Until Death Do Us Part

On June 9, 2021, Casey and Cassandra were married in Asheville at Looking Glass Falls. It was an outdoor wedding, and the bride was insistent that the wedding would proceed rain or shine from this exact location. The night before the forecast was showing a strong possibility of rain in the morning. It was a 75 percent chance to be exact! The night before, Pastor Sam prayed for sunshine. On the evening before the wedding, the waterfall was a bit dirty looking from previous rains earlier in the day. The wedding party settled in at the Clarion Inn.

The next morning and day of the wedding, we gathered in the morning but in separate rooms as the bride and groom prepared to be wed. As I was walking down the hallway with the photographer to their rooms, we glanced outside to see a beautiful cardinal perched on a window ledge. The beautiful bird caught the corner of my eye. I remember my mother saying, "If I return to earth, I want to come back as a cardinal." Well, it seemed to me it was a bit odd to see one at that exact moment. Was this an accident or sighting from the heavens?

As the bride was getting ready, she announced that her family did not have her veil. A bride dreams of the perfect wedding, and it includes the bridal gown and veil. However, in the process of packing to make the four-hour trip to the mountains, the veil was forgotten. This was a moment of disappointment for the bride-to-be, but we tried to console her as best we could. The focus was on the ceremony and the union, not the veil. She took a deep breath and very graciously accepted the current situation. Her dad felt so bad that he drove over to a bridal shop to see if he could find a replacement.

It was just not meant to be. Cassandra put on a crown instead of a veil and proceeded to get ready, mustering the attitude of a bride that would not let anything stop her from being wed on that day. Hannah, the photographer, captured memories throughout the process to capture the sweetness of the big day.

As the wedding party stepped outside to prepare to leave, we noticed the sun shining! Amazing! God answered our prayers, and we were grateful! We picked up the flowers from the florist and headed to Looking Glass Falls. The hour had come, but we were not prepared for the number of people at a State Park on a Wednesday in the middle of the week! Tourists were everywhere at the falls. We politely told them we are preparing for a wedding. We told them the ceremony would only take a few minutes and asked if they would please wait to see the waterfall and enjoy the park after we finished the ceremony. We proceeded to put balloons up to mark the stairs where the bride would walk down. With no internet signal or Wi-Fi, we could not play the song the bride picked out. The procession began with Steve and I, Tonya, mother of the bride, and lastly, Cassandra and her dad John. Pastor Sam and ring bearer Brandon were already in place in the water.

The symbolism of the jagged rocks and crevices that led to the beautiful site were significant from the perspective of the bride and groom. The jagged rocks over time had been cleansed with the constant flow of rushing water. The water was no longer dirty from the previous day's rain. The terrain was both treacherous and dangerous to navigate. The years leading up to this day had been uncertain and dangerous at times. Their paths leading up to this day were paved with jagged edges just like the rocks. The rushing water from the waterfall represents the cleansing and renewing of their relationship over time. The symbolism is beautiful and real! Cassandra navigated the slippery rocks like a champ, and Casey grabbed her hand to bring her safely to the water's edge of the waterfall. The waterfall was crystal clear, and the sun shimmered down on it. The setting was amazing. The journey over the rocks and slippery stones was symbolism of their relationship up to this point! What a beautiful narrative and story. To say their relationship was rocky, unstable, and unpredictable was an understatement. I understood in that moment why they needed to be in the water closest to the waterfall. The stones represented a past life, and the water represented a new life. The imagery of the clear waterfall was an important piece of their story. I had a light bulb moment when I clearly understood the bride's unwavering desire to be wed at that very site, and I immediately felt it was perfect.

Pastor Sam recited his part as officiator, and Casey and Cassandra stated their handwritten and crafted with love vows to each other. Their favorite scriptures were read. The first was from **John 15:5: "I am the vine; you are the branches if you remain in me and I in you, he it is that bears much fruit, for apart from me you can do nothing"** (NIV). This verse represented who Casey and Cassandra are in the Lord because of their commitment to him. Her favorite verse from **1 Corinthians 13:4 was read after that: "Love is patient, love is kind…"** The ring bearer, Brandon, handed the box Casey's grandmother gave him with the rings inside and a picture of his grandparents nestled in the very bottom. The music box played "Amazing Grace," her favorite hymn. Casey is very sentimental and insisted on using that box and having a picture displayed on a chair as if both grandparents were present for the ceremony. Even if his dear grandparents could not be there physically, they could watch from the heavenly realm and have a front row seat. The ceremony lasted less than thirty minutes, but it was the beginning of a lifelong commitment. The tourists who were standing on the rocks observed the big day. They cheered and clapped for Casey and Cassandra. People were very respectful and had no idea they would be a witness to a beautiful wedding under the waterfall.

Before leaving Looking Glass Falls that day, Casey and Cassandra planted a tree in honor of their union as one at the very site. They will go back on anniversaries and visit again to hopefully find the tree still alive and thriving in the park as a symbol of their love for each other. As they both were about to leave the park, another cardinal made an appearance. It stayed close to the area where Casey and Cassandra planted the tree. Casey and Cassandra noticed it and said, "This is Grandma looking over us and giving us her blessing from heaven." Casey and Cassandra are convinced that the second sighting of a cardinal was a symbol of the goodness of God and his grandma's sweet spirit. After all, Catherine Greene Brannon was the force behind helping them through rough times and molding their faith in God! The cardinal's appearance represented devotion, a loving relationship, and monogamy. Some believe that cardinals appear when angels are near, perhaps as a sweet, unexpected visitor from heaven.

Within an hour of returning to the Clarion Inn for the reception, rain poured from the clouds that had formed. Rumor has it that if it rains on your wedding day, it is good luck for many years together as husband and wife. The Bible states in **Isaiah 44:3–4, "For I will pour water on a thirsty land and streams on the dry ground. I will pour out my spirit on your offspring and blessings on your descendants. They will spring up like grass on a meadow like poplar trees from flowing streams"** (ESV).

Many people who know Casey and Cassandra doubted they would ever have a healthy relationship and would never get married, but God had a different plan. His plan is recorded in **Jeremiah 29:11: "For I know the plans I have for you,' declares the Lord, 'plans to prosper you and not to harm you, plans to give you hope and a future"** (NIV). God has a good plan for Casey and Cassandra if they make him first in their marriage.

This special day, with its symbolism everywhere from the sunshine, water, terrain, the cardinal, the rings, and the rain pronounced God's grace and faithfulness. Some may call these little incidences coincidences, but we know that God provided the symbols to remind us of his presence. Because Casey and Cassandra committed their lives to him, they were blessed by him on their wedding day.

Is this the fairy-tale ending that all the readers want to imagine, or will their life together be challenging and rocky like the jagged rocks and slippery slope leading down to the waterfall? I will leave that question unanswered for the one who holds their future in his hands.

Epilogue

It has been well over a year since I started the journey of writing this book, and I have learned some valuable lessons along the way. It has been a healing journey, and my eyes have become wide open to reality and the truth. The truth is that it has taken me so long to write this book because there have been setbacks along the way. Some relationships I cherish have shifted and been pushed to the side, and some have been compromised. It has been a struggle at times to focus, and I have delayed, questioned, and doubted myself along the way. My faith is what has sustained me and pushed me forward. God has reminded me of the importance of this book and the many people who could be impacted. I have encountered every roadblock and even considered not publishing the book at all because of the turmoil it has caused in my life. Quitting in the face of adversity is not an option for me because I have put my heart and soul into this book, and I am excited to see how God will use it to bless others.

Conclusion

Casey had developed an unhealthy habit of taking a substance when things were uncomfortable, awkward, or painful at an early age. As an addict, this was the go-to solution. Now as a young adult, he is learning to cope with life circumstances in a more productive and healthy way. Honestly, I know the Bible says as Christians, we have to forgive seventy times seven times, but I feel like that I am very close to meeting that quota. Forgiveness is for the person who has been offended even if the perpetrator does not ask for forgiveness.

I think I have forgiven Casey for many things, but I will never forget unless my memory is wiped clean. God has taught me to *love* unconditionally and to forgive my son for all of his transgressions. But with the gift of forgiveness, I had to create boundaries to protect myself and examine my own heart and motivation. If I am honest, this has been an internal struggle that would manifest itself in different ways in my life. At times, the sadness and feeling of hopelessness was overwhelming. My Savior felt distant, and unanswered prayers were frustrating.

I realize now that my God was shaping and molding me to be the person I am today. In unexpected ways, he sent people to encourage me and comfort me. One of those people was my dear sweet mother. She was always a listening ear and shoulder to cry on. I spent many hours with her, and I am so thankful for her life and legacy. She always made me feel hopeful in different ways. She was my biggest supporter, and honestly, she treated me more like a friend than a daughter. I admire her life and legacy she left behind, and I want to shine my light the way she did.

My personal struggles do not define me, but they have shaped me, and I have learned what faith truly is. As a result, I have been able to be that empathetic listener who does not judge others. At times, in this season, I always felt like others were judging me and silently saying, "Why are you continuing to support your son?" You are an enabler, and you are not helping him! The voices, whether audible or not, were always present in my ear.

I always questioned my decisions and reactions. I did my best to remain calm and not overreact. There was one thing that remained constant, and that was the unconditional love for my one and only son. I just longed for a healthy relationship with my son. Was that asking so much? I do not want any mother, or family member to feel like I did, alone in your own misery with no *hope* in sight. This is my real motivation for writing this book. If I lived through this and came out on the other side with my sanity intact and a healthy relationship with my adult son, then you can too.

In the last phase of the refining process for the pearl, God puts his print there to remind Casey he is a child of the highest God, and that is all that truly matters.

It would be disrespectful and hypocritical for me to say that my son's story is over. He conquered the monster and won the war! We can claim victory and move on with our lives. The truth is, this is an ongoing struggle for my son, Casey, and most addicts. Those who fought hard and still lost the battle, I have great empathy for you as I have walked this uncertain road with you. The truth is, the addict can make strides and get better for a period of time and still find that he or she has to continually, every minute of every day, be reminded to choose life over addiction. Relapse is always a possibility and real threat to any addict trying to do better and make a better life. For those families left behind with broken hearts and dreams, I am so extremely sorry. I hope you will turn your pain into purpose and fight for those addicts and be a support for the families. There are so many who have to go on through life every day with the reality that the person they loved and cherished is no longer present. Please be a voice as I will for those who still fight this *monster* and are barely hanging on to hope.

The parable in the Bible of the lost sheep comes to mind as I reflect on this journey. Jesus is our shepherd, and we are his sheep. Jesus tells the story of leaving the ninety-nine in search of the one lost sheep. Casey was once a lost sheep, but now he is found.

Endorsements

It has been my honor to witness the development and transformation of my friend, Casey Ennis. From addiction and hopelessness, Casey and his family have "hit bottom" several times! Yet the two most powerful loves in the world—God's love and the love of a parent—never faded. In this book, you will find tragedy, destruction, brokenness, and heartbreak. However, you will also find hope, salvation, redemption, and reconciliation!

If you or someone you know is battling with addictions and hopelessness, *read this book*!

It is my prayer that the same love and redemption that has come to the entire Ennis family will be found in your life also. And that you too will discover "the pearl in your own oyster!"

> Pastor Sam Stovall
> Next Steps Pastor
> Quest Fellowship Church

Wow! What an amazing book of God's supernatural work in and through the life of an addict and his family who survived the horrific experiences and effects of chemical addictions! God has used C.B. Ennis and her family in a mighty way to share very openly and honestly from the core of their hearts and emotions to encourage and help people through their overwhelmingly horrible experiences from the evils of chemical addictions! If you or someone you love or know is experiencing chemical addictions and the daily chaos and powerless feelings from this disease, you need to read this book immediately and share it with others for help, strength, encouragement, and life-saving advice!

>Rodger and Janet Sauls, Cofounders,
>2 Become 1 Ministries

This book has the power to help families who have loved ones who are living with addictions to know they are not alone, and there is help. This book can also help friends and neighbors have a little window into the lives of family and friends who may be living with this nightmare. In turn, I believe the pages of this book will lead many to action as support and as prayer warriors for those walking through addictions. The heart-wrenching story of a family who fought hard is written on the pages of this book. The love, grace, and forgiveness of our loving God is threaded throughout their story, and it has a beautiful ending.

>Susan T. Smith
>English Professor

References

1994. *The Experiencing God Bible.* New International Version. Broadman & Holloman.
2011. *Rooted.* Zondervan.

About the Author

C.B. Ennis is a wife and mother of two. She is a former educator as well. She was inspired to write this book because the monster, addiction, entered the lives of the Ennis family unexpectedly and without warning.

Addiction is a family disease, and they had to stand united to fight back against the evil. At the time they were experiencing this, there was no literature or self-help books that helped them navigate this unfamiliar territory. So they decided to share their own very personal story with the world and what seemed to work for them in hoping to save some lives and give hope to the hopeless.

C.B. Ennis has many interests that include bike riding, kayaking, traveling, spending time with family and friends, and landscaping.